I0233135

Reflections:

LIFE'S POEMS AND OTHER STORIES

Nina Olsson

G
H
P

Grosvenor House
Publishing Limited

All rights reserved
Copyright © Nina Olsson, 2019

The right of Nina Olsson to be identified as the author of this
work has been asserted in accordance with Section 78
of the Copyright, Designs and Patents Act 1988

The book cover is copyright to Nina Olsson

This book is published by
Grosvenor House Publishing Ltd
Link House
140 The Broadway, Tolworth, Surrey, KT6 7HT.
www.grosvenorhousepublishing.co.uk

This book is sold subject to the conditions that it shall not, by way of
trade or otherwise, be lent, resold, hired out or otherwise circulated
without the author's or publisher's prior consent in any form of binding or
cover other than that in which it is published and
without a similar condition including this condition being imposed
on the subsequent purchaser.

A CIP record for this book
is available from the British Library

ISBN 978-1-78623-635-7

This book is dedicated to all of those I have known,
and those I have yet to know.

Inspiration taken from all.

Photographic Plates and Illustrations

Photographs:

1. Reflections - Albert Dock Boats, Liverpool, UK
2. Shoreline   - Evening at Rock Ferry, Wirral, UK
3. Sunset   - New Brighton Skies , Wirral, UK

Illustrations:

1. Angel Wings
2. Beach
3. Bullets
4. Cheese
5. Dragon
6. Feather
7. Le Chat
8. Needle
9. Poppy
10. Storm Cloud
11. Telephone
12. The Letter
13. The River
14. The Train
15. Scattered Leaves

All Photographs by Nina Olsson
All Illustrations by Lez Harvey
Cover Artwork by Lez Harvey

Reflections:

'Change in the direction of a wave front
at an interface. Commonly light, sound
and water.

- Echoes in acoustics.
- Light images sent back from mirrored surfaces.
- Contemplation or a long consideration. Interpretation
  of what is going on between thinking and learning.
- The opportunity to gain self-knowledge.'

Collins English Dictionary

Preface

Life holds many surprises for us all, some good, some unpleasant, some awkward and some very happy.

I have had such a life, one on which I can look back and say with a couple of notable exceptions, that I have no regrets. I have achieved most of what I wanted to do, although, of course, there are still many new adventures awaiting.

I have seen places, met amazing people, loved some, lost some, and in some cases simply misplaced them, drifting apart over time.

An ordinary life, but at times extraordinary. I have learnt from all whom I have met, and hope some have learnt from me.

These observations were written over several decades, reminiscences from the height of the 'Troubles', from hospital beds, from the arms of lovers and from many joyous times.

So, where now? Well, anywhere the mood and circumstance take me.

I hope that you will do the same.

Nina xxx

Contents

Life's
Poems

My Name is who I am

Am I completely me
Or parts of many others
Does the face that looks out to the world
Really resemble the face that is within
I am, or am I
Who am I,
My name is who I am.

Take me as I am,
But can you find the real me,
What lies beneath this outside,
Which thoughts come forth to say,
This is me,
But who is me,
My name is who I am

Mother

Inside your body, I began my life,
The centre of your very being,
And for that while, you knew nothing of me,
Only that I was there.

Always a part of you, my first breath,
Made you part of me,
Fed on love, and watered with your tears,
You taught me to live and grow.

How our bond suffered in those later years,
So much I wanted to see,
So many things I had to do,
Believing you understood little of my life.

Now, that my child is part of me,
I've learnt how much you gave,
You stood, behind me, beyond me, beside me,
Patiently waiting for the bond to heal.

Questions

Pens and letters, what are they writing,
Scribbles and doodles, on paper are seen,
Soldiers in far off countries are fighting,
Who can tell me, what does it all mean.

Cars are travelling, petrol they're burning,
Ambulances arriving at an accident scene,
Scholars, in schools, are steadily learning,
Who can tell me, what does it all mean.

In the streets, the people are talking,
Discussing the TV programmes they've seen,
In the parks, the children are playing,
Who can tell me, what does it all mean.

Guards, in front of the Palace, are changing,
Visitors, hoping to glimpse the Queen,
Politicians, are our lives rearranging,
Who can tell me, what does it all mean.

Farmers, the seeds are busily sowing,
Later, all the harvest to glean,
Leaves, before the wind are blowing,
Who can tell me, what does it all mean.

Who, is all the answers supplying,
Where do we go, where have we been,
Loving, crying, living and dying,
Who can tell me, what does it all mean?

He is my day

He is my day,
We lie in sleep together,
He moves, gently his hand caresses my naked body,
Our bodies merge to become one joyful pool,
Then once more we sleep.

He is my afternoon,
The telephone rings,
He speaks gentle words of love and encouragement,
Then asks what's for tea,
How like a man, my man.

He is my evening,
We sit en-rapt in our own thoughts,
Occasionally speaking of the days events,
Secure in our love,
and understanding.

He is my night,
Our bed warm like a mother's womb,
We lie sleepily,
Happy that all is well with us,
We say goodnight and sleep like babes.

My Son

In a cot, at the bottom of my bed,
There lies a child,
A wonderful being, given to me,
Lovingly by his father.

This child is my sun,
He fills my life with rays of hope and happiness,
He stirs,
Such a wonderful combination of skin and bones,
No man could put together such a complex puzzle.

His mind so eager to be filled with thoughts,
Some mine, some his, some from all he meets,
He lies sleeping, waiting for experience to awaken him,
To teach him the mysteries of life.

My sun, my moon, my child,
Born of me to be shared with the world,
His freedom ready to be sampled, slowly, deeply,
I'll hold him not, he belongs to life.

Incommunicado

I sat in a room full of people,
And yet I was alone,
Wrapt in my thoughts, as they were in theirs,
All of them on their phones..

Mrs Jones died last week,
Oh, poor soul, (Who was she?)
No-one seemed to be interested,
Is this how life is to be?

Don't involve yourself with others,
Don't let their troubles be unfurled,
No love, no joy, no understanding,
Isolated in your own little world.

REFLECTIONS

I can see you there,
Lurking in my mirror,
What do you want from me?
I have nothing to offer,
No great deeds,
No great joy,
Only my soul in it's earthly shell.

Physical beauty have you not,
And yet, each line
Carved deeply into your face,
Tells of pleasure and of pain,
Experiences many,
Happiness some,
I do not know you, yet recognition dawns

There in your eyes, a strange reflection,
A faint remembrance,
There builds in me a feeling,
It's weakness in each moment passing,
The years were cruel,
Nature had her revenge,
But your flame still flickers in the dark.

I close my eyes, but you're not gone,
Still watching from my mirror,
What do you want from me,
My soul is all I have,
We two are one,
And I am you,
There is no comfort from the cold glass stare.

Colours

It's grey today,
Grey skies and grey here,
Here inside me,
Sometimes light clouds pass, hurrying on their way,
I reach out and touch them,
But they turn to grey in my hands.

It's blue today,
A light, bright blueness,
All around me,
Circles of brightness light up my horizons,
I reach out into the warmth,
And the sun sits in my hands.

It's red today,
A heavy uneasy red,
I cannot break through crimson bonds,
They burn and hurt me,
I reach out to break them,
But they turn to chain in my hands.

It's white today,
A blank, stark white,
There is no beginning or end,
I'm floating,
I reach out to feel it,
But it turns to infinity in my hands.

Inside the Inside

Help me, help me to climb out,
Out of this plastic bubble,
I can see you, hear you,
But not touch you.

The sides breathe and squeeze me,
Deeper and deeper inside,
You are still there, talking and smiling,
Can't you see?

Hold out your hand, can you not feel,
This moving skin, clinging around me,
Break through it, let me out,
It only bends to my touch.

It is so bright in here, and such flashes,
Beautiful flashes of rainbow colour,
There is no night and day,
Only now, now, now.

I'm choking, liquid plastic covers me,
Still you talk on, don't you hear?
The air is still now, I see you move,
With slow dreamlike movements.

Call me, call me, call me again,
But I am not here,
I have become a plastic bubble,
Floating ever away from you.

Half-forgotten paths

How careless is our mind's wanderings,
Cannoning down paths of unfulfilled dreams,
Tearing open the heart's treasured packets,
Spilling their contents to life's cold view.

So much time spent storing dreams and hopes,
Each logged into memory, with a place of it's own,
And those too special, placed in the heart's domain,
To be kept until their pain had healed.

Too tired now, to offer resistance,
I let you rush down half-forgotten paths,
Content to drift along in yesterday's glory,
Until the thoughts bring remembered pain and tears.

But wait, a light begins to flicker,
Gathering strength, until shining bright,
The good memories, happy memories, love and laughter,
Promise of paths yet to come.

Faded Plumage

Proud Peacock, sparkling from your bar stool,
Jewels of wit falling from your lips,
Don't you know, they no longer listen,
All those men you once drew to your flame.

The 30s belle, with your Parkeresque mind,
The centre of your social circle,
What happened in those years between,
Whilst they grew old. And what of you

You, in your middle-aged body, but with siren's need,
Does not your mirror now tell you the truth?
The once admiring looks, now tinged with sorrow and disgust,
Proud, proud, faded bird.

The Boy on the Beach

Like an echo of my youth,
You came stealing into my life,
Reminding me of a time gone by,
A lifestyle almost forgotten.

You reached into my soul, and left there
An emptiness craving to be filled,
Through your dreams I lived again mine.

Such a short meeting, how could it have touched me so deeply,
Yet, it has,
Transporting me back to another time, another me,
Before life had taken it's toll.

Come again, fill my heart with your music,
Take me back through time,
Touch me with your words,
Touch me with your enthusiasm,
And let me live again with the fire of youthful dreams.

Unhappy Country

Oh, unhappy country,
With your babes beating on your breast,
No womb warmth for thee,
Your life's blood, ebbing away
with each turn of the tide.

Open up your arms,
And take in love,
Unhappy country,
Life is all around you,
Yet only in death do you rejoice,
Fill your soul with hope, and let peace grow.

Time cannot heal all,
Without compassion in your heart,
Oh, unhappy country,
Cast your green skirts around you,
And bring your children back home.

Take your first breath of a new life,
Let each do what brings joy,
Unhappy country,
In love you were born,
Now hate waits with outstretched arms.

My heart grieves for you,
Proud, unhappy country,
Your sons die, and your daughters weep,
Happiness a feeling, dimly remembered,
Whilst death sits on your knee.

I love you, my country,
No boundaries mark my heart,
You are as a woman now,
With children gone from home,
Sad and lonely and old.

Requiem for a future lost

You, with your pipes and drums,
Call you the dead from their sleep,
or the living to their death?
Let this soul lie in peace,
Bring not the blackness down on
the heads of the innocents.

Life is precious,
Think more of those left behind,
The children cry in the night,
Understanding not, the ideals,
Understanding not, the history,
Knowing only the relentless present.

Procession after procession,
March down through the years.
With Death always holding the mace,
Let the dead sleep, disturb not their rest,
Let the past heal, and give life to the now.

Faint Sighs and Muffled Shots

Talk to me, sad country
Tell me what pain you bear,
I cannot see what went before,
What is locked away in your heart.

I have tried to reach down,
Moving aside the layers of this time,
To those dark days,
Many years ago.

I have opened up my ears,
But hear only distant sounds,
Faint sighs and muffled shots,
And languages unknown to me.

Shadows steal across the fields,
Are they real?
Or ghosts of the past,
Come again to claim the land.

I have so much to ask you,
Help me to understand,
What happened, when so much was said,
So little done.

Each leader believing in the cause,
Where are they now?
Do they still listen with fire in their breasts,
Helpless, whilst people makes the same mistakes.

Talk to me, sad country,
Tell me of your pain,
Your wounds are covered, but not healed,
And still the hurt goes on.

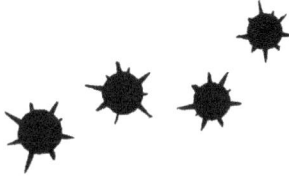

Scottish Soldier's Lament

1981

If you cross the sea to this land,
Be sure that at the ending of your day,
There's not a gunman waiting with a bullet,
To lay you in the fields so far away.

I always wanted to join the Army,
Travel the world, see what I could see,
But now they've sent me out to these streets,
In places I least wanted to be.

The young girls all come to you a'smiling,
With gentle words of love upon their breath,
But they are only messengers for others,
To lure you very gently to you death.

They say they're fighting in the name o' Jesus,
Protestant against the Catholic,
Our problem's solved while playing football,
When Rangers are at home to Celtic.

Of course, my view is so simplistic,
The problem is more complex than that,
Land divisions, votes and pride in nation,
The history, that is on all heads, sat.

So if you go across the sea to that land,
Be sure that at the ending of your day,
There's not a gunman waiting with a bullet,
To lay you in those green fields far away.

Clusters of Black Sequins

What is this thing growing inside me,
Growing cell by cell,
Possessing all that comes within it's grasp,
I feel nothing,
I see nothing,
Until I become it, and not it, me.

Rays bombard me,
Killing my beauty, my dignity, but not it,
Such hope I had,
But the doubts grew, as the thing within me,
It consumes me, from the inside out,
But still I feel nothing.

Now, when I am looking thin and old,
Now comes the pain,
Such pain as never before experienced,
Kind faces tell me there is always hope,
I tell me, but the thing feeds on,
Growing, growing, growing.

So foolish was I,
A few minutes spared then, would now have spared me,
Pain is mine, but more to those I love,
More to those who wait,
The battle you've won, cold unfeeling thing,
But with me, you die.

Another Day

The glorious sun awoke me this morning,
Well, that and a thermometer in my mouth,
I made it, this far anyway,
Wonder if they will tell what they've found.

Yesterday, I was so afraid,
Of the test, anaesthetic and of dying,
Tomorrow, I may still die,
But I'll have the brightness of today.

No results? No not yet,
Don't worry, they kindly say,
How, not to worry, when my future
lies on a glass slide in some laboratory.

I'm so selfish of my life,
For my family and for me,
My heart desperately tries to hope,
Whilst my head loudly screams.

Another day, and then I'll know,
Which way the pendulum has swung,
Am I brave enough to take the truth,
Of what I never thought would happen to me.

The Letter

It came today, my darling,
The letter,
The one we talked about, worried about,
And hoped would never come.

It is with deepest regret,
Such stark words, crying out,
From paper so white, so pure,
It's black border, crushing my heart.

So few words, was brave, well liked,
But what do they say of you,
Your life enclosed in two lines of ink,
But there was more, much more.

What do they say of your spirit,
Of dreams, or fears and doubts,
Of long days spent walking,
Warm nights of love, in our bed.

It came today, my darling,
The letter that ended hope,
I'll try to be brave, my darling,
And hold you forever within me.

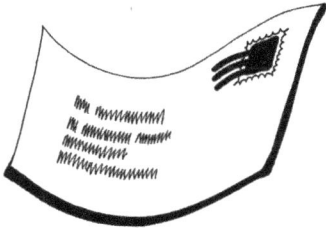

Life's Battlefield

Is this war within me, real or of my imagining?
Such turmoil of spirit,
Weakens me,
Yet in that weakness,
Lies an unknown strength,
Reaching out.

Here lies peace and tranquillity,
Here lies hope,
Here they lie, are the dead?
No, not dead, only sleeping,
Shell-shocked and bleeding,
Afraid.

Faceless and formless they float,
Aimless and wanting,
Though in some dark passage,
Lies Love,
Waiting to flower, bright and clean,
New.

An Apple for the Innocent

Come sweet Eve, come,
See what pearls I can off,
Life is so full, such joy,
Such pleasures I alone can give you.

Come sweet Eve, come,
Look into my crystal eyes,
Here are men who wait to adore you,
Yours to command and use.

Come sweet Eve, come,
I'll show you all life's mysteries,
The minds to conquer, ambitions to fire,
Take from all, they are yours.

Come sweet Eve, come,
Let not your innocence hold you back,
I'll teach you how to live,
Evil's such a succulent prize.

Come sweet Eve, come,
Stay not in his garden,
He cannot give you such joy as I,
Come, be free of earthly bonds.

Come sweet Eve, come,
Take one bite, one deep bite,
Forbidden fruit is so much sweeter,
Come join your soul with mine.

Come sweet Eve, come,
The journey is not so hard,
Once that first step you've taken,
And oh, what pleasures wait for you.

Come sweet Eve, come,
Cower not at his wrath,
You are lost to him forever,
Is not your life gloriously free.

Come sweet Eve, come,
Weep not at what is gone,
Innocence can never last, I called you,
and like a gentle lamb you came.

Come sweet Eve, come,
Turn not again to him,
I am stronger, feel my power,
Eve, my Eve, WHY HAVE YOU LEFT ME?

Alfred

I cannot see you old,
You are forever young, within mine eye,
No lines of life have yet marked your face,
Though warmth and knowledge linger there.

I did not know you,
But how I wish that had been true,
Could we have met in some country lane,
With raised hat, you'd pass me by.

I've dreamed, whilst in your words I've bathed,
Reaching out to touch you with my mind,
I've waited by the sparkling brook,
Where the golden wheat did softly blow.

I cannot shed the heavy years,
My world, would to you such sorrow bring,
I am, but a child, in this cold game of life,
Searching for comfort in your domain.

With eyelids closed, I think of you,
Down through time my feelings run,
Stand by the gate, and wait for me,
Oh, I see you, and you are beautiful.

Child of Yesterday

You look uneasy child,
Dressed in your fancy clothes,
I know what lies behind that troubled face,
For I too have travelled that lonely path.

Poor forgotten child, life is hard for you,
And eases none, as time goes by,
Feeling outside, so far from what's real,
Trapped in a time, seventy years too late.

How many languorous afternoons had you spent,
Where sunlit waters, from the fountains danced,
How often did you walk with friends, who laughed
with such gaiety now seldom heard.

Other children taunt you, hurt you, but are afraid,
Of your ways, and how you see your life,
They do not understand, in your child's body,
There is another time, trying to be free.

They wonder at your knowledge, such fine detail,
But you were there, weren't you,
You live, their past, your present,
You know what pain the future brings.

Poor child, life is hard for you,
Looking unhappy in your fancy clothes,
I too have lived with that feeling,
I understand, and pity you.

Is this really Love (I)

Should I tell you how much I love you,
Would you smile, and would that beautiful smile fade
with the feelings of constraint that enter your heart,
You are so beautiful,
Your mouth warm and sensuous,
Paroxysms of pleasure, cascade through me,
Just looking at you.

I loved you very much,
But will keep that love closed inside me,
It threatened you, perhaps hurt you,
I am sorry for both of us,
Wasted time, when time was so precious,
Was this really love?
Do we ever really know.

Part of me hungers for you still,
Though mind or body, I know not which,
Take me to your heart,
Let me be one with you,
Don't push me from your warmth.

Was it so wrong, our love?
Were the years too many to bear,
I cannot deeply sleep,
In waking I dream,
Longing to be with you again.

Is this really Love (II)

I've sat and tried to put you into words,
But I cannot,
You are as elusive as one drop of water,
Flowing in a river,
You drift like the mist,
Swirling, and staying nowhere.

I love you,
I think it's love,
But it is so destructive,
I listen as you speak of someone else,
Smiling, as I fall apart inside,
Is this really love?

Sometimes I see you in the night,
I reach out
and just as I think I touch you,
You are gone,
I have sat and tried to put you into words,
But am left with only tears.

You are the opium of my soul.

Is this really Love (III)

Now tomorrow is today,
Why do I love you?
Eleven o'clock,
Alone,
No, not alone,
You are in my thoughts,
I wish you weren't,
Life is never simple.

Why, when people love each other,
Is there such pain,
Such turmoil,
I saw myself in the mirror,
Could that really be me,
So strained, so tired,
Yet when we are together,
I feel such joy.

Joy, pain, sadness,
Deep, deep sadness,
Crying out silently, my very soul aches,
I feel as if my light is going out,
Is this really love?
There must be more than this,
And yet without such sorrow,
How can we measure what is good.

You hide behind a powdered veil,
Lifted, it crumbles in my hand,
How much of the dust is you?
I have given all that I can,

But for both of us, it is not enough,
Am I destroying you?
Keeping you in that unreal world,
Feeling safe, though you have fallen over the edge.

Do I love you enough to let you go,
Who will catch me, when I fall,
Is this really love?
This cannot be all there is,
Time seeming to hold it's breath,
But in reality screaming by,
Leaving us behind,
Tomorrow has become today.

Addiction

I couldn't compete with her,
She was his first love,
Oh, I tried,
But she would call, and away he would go,
In the middle of the night,
On a summer's day, in the country,
She'd always be there,
Whispering in his ear,
Calling him softly, insistently.

I loved him so much,
But she always claimed him,
My body warm and waiting,
Would wait on through the night,
She devoured him and left nothing for me.
How I hated her,
For what she made him, for what she made me,
We all suffered, and still he was hers.

Somewhere in Time

The past came to meet me today,
Not how you would imagine,
Not noisily, but quietly, slowly, picking away,
Each little layer of hidden truths.

Little secrets, but secrets no more,
Some parts even unknown to me,
Well, not unknown but forgotten,
Hidden in the depths of memory.

When youth confronts the older you,
Consequences force their way,
Into the conscious thoughts,
Of what was, and now will ever be.

Who is affected, who must really care,
Lives now forever altered,
For once it is known, it is never unknown,
No going back to change what is there.

No regrets, no, no regrets,
From there comes, a much loved and cherished time,
A time of being, here and now,
Present and past made whole again.

Quiet

'Cloud bathing at Nina's place, talks of lionesses and cubs'

The day came, when the house was so quiet,
It wasn't always so,
Filled with music, laughter and noise,
Young people, sometimes many,
Sometimes few,
Drinking the coffee,
Made from the list by the door,
Talking of all that was new in their world.

Somewhere to gather when Youth Theatre was done,
A meeting place, to relax amongst friends,
Airing their views,
Sharing their news,
Conversations aplenty,
Playing their songs and singing aloud,
On makeshift instruments, pots and pans,
Or rehearsing their parts for the next Show.

Three decades have passed, and where are they now,
Those happy, creative, talented people,
Their teenage years long gone,
They have all moved on,
Children and jobs,
Day to day living,
But with good memories, many,
Their own homes filled with laughter and song.

Angels

I see Angels, wherever I look,
Oh, not the winged kind,
Though they are there, I'm sure,
At the front, the back and sides of you,
Watching out, guiding your way.

These are more the abstract kind, there if you look,
A track side pipe, clasped hands and wings,
A large statue with outstretched arms,
A shadow on a building, an ethereal shape,
A carving lovingly guarding a grave.

An angel in uniform, there when you wake,
From what life throws at you,
Or just waking from sleep,
There to embrace you, enfold you
And tell you you're safe.

Shapes in the clouds, shapes on the ground,
In people who love you,
In family and friends,
In beliefs, in books, or just in your mind,
Angels before you, beside you and behind.

Albums

I sorted through my albums,
Into places that I had been,
Memories made, moments captured in time,
People and places,
Some forgotten, some fresh in my mind.

Places that I have visited, revisited and seen,
Others that are no longer there,
Ravaged by war, or by politics,
Barriers created, now access denied,
But their populaces hopeful as they ever have been.

Jungles and beaches, cities and lakes,
Scenes of devastation, dirt and poverty,
But also renewal, conservation and new builds,
In awe inspiring, breath-taking scenery,
Begging to be seen.

Ornate Churches, buildings old and new,
Baroque, Victorian, Modern to name just a few,
Famous landmarks, bridges and man-made wonders,
Towers and housing, landscapes and river fronts,
Reflecting their time and place when first on view.

Peoples from many nations, different sizes and hue,
Locals, visitors, and sightseers passing through,
Many forms of transport, Cars, Boats and Trains,
Sleds, Rickshaws, Trams and Planes,
On foot, in city streets, surveying the scenes.

Stories, like scattered leaves,
Blown to the edges of memory,
Their colours ever changing as seasons come and go,
Waiting whilst new sights and sounds,
To take their place in my diaries of life.

With my cup of tea, I sit,
And let my mind wander back through time,
A life full of pictures, and tales now told,
Experiences many, and still some to come,
Lessons from life, on my book shelves.

Old Friends

Old friends can be naughty,
Some can be nice,
Some can be distant,
Others be near,
And some forever holding you dear.

Time does not a good friend make,
Some, made in a moment, are a lifetime to last,
Some seem like friends, a surface veneer,
But not real friends, there for you,
For ever and ever.

A two-way street, one to the other,
On sunny days, and those that are darker,
Friends are defenders, and champions all,
Your fun time companions, travel mates,
There for your holidays and hospital dates.

A mutual time of love and respect,
Not always agreeing, and right that should be,
Cared for and nurtured, each to the other,
A friendship through time, with give and take,
Friendships that last whatever may happen.

Rock Savage

Lights in the dark,
The darkness made light,
A forest of steel,
Glistening and bright.

Castles on the landscape,
Turrets stark against the sky,
Where Knights may be searching,
And Dragons fly high.

Look, can you see them?
Their tongues shooting flame,
Lighting up the blackness,
A moment, then darkness again.

A place full of legend,
Of mystery and lore,
A magical kingdom,
Till Dawn opens her door.

A forest of steel,
Glistening and bright,
With all of it's secrets,
Awaiting the next night.

JCB

Like some pre-historic beast she sits,
Large eyes glimmering in the sun,
Blinking as she whines in the face of the dawn,
Spasms rock her from within,
Groaning deeply,
Until she bursts, roaring, to meet the day.

Lumbering forward at speeds belieing her bulk,
Roaring, squealing, choking,
Clouds of smoke forming a halo over her head,
With delicate violence, she tears a nest in the ground,
Moving, shifting, layer from layer,
Mother Earth unceremoniously dis-robed.

Are you progress? Tearing open
all that lies in your path,
Leaving no stone unturned,
Are you cleansing, changing life,
Pulling down the old,
Turning the new inside out.

But how long till you, like the Dinosaurs,
Are totally extinct,
Leaving fossils, rusting in the ground,
To show you ever were,
Now with your day's work done,
Like some pre-historic beast you sit,
Dark against the sky.

The Lost Rhyme

How often have I sat and waited,
For inspiration to fill my head,
How many half completed lines of rhyme,
Lie forsaken, discarded, dead.

The perfect first line, the second profound,
The words tumbling on to the page,
Then spaces, odd letters and doodles,
And within me, frustration and rage.

I've read books, joined in writer's circles,
But still it comes out the same,
Bare titles, lost words on clean paper,
I've tried, should I try again?

Blue Light

Yesterday

Had a thrill,
With Phil,
What a buzz,
It really wuzz,
Blue Light,
Knuckle fright,
Out of sight,
Land slide,
Rover ride,
Front to sit,
Adrenaline hit,
Siren's wailing,
My face pale-ing.

Action horn,
Kicking up a storm.
Red light jumping,
My heart bumping,
Cars apace,
Making space,
Road race,

Crossing feet,
Grip the seat,
Police waiting,
Escort making,
Under the river,
It's now or never,
Platelet carrying life-giver,

Arrowe Park,
Nearly dark,
Patient needy,
Delivery speedy,
Eight minutes, door to door,
I like it,
Give me more.

Army lives and Army Wives

If you love and marry a soldier,
You must be prepared, 'til the service ends,
For excitement, upheaval and travel,
Away from your family and friends.

From the Napoleonic wars onwards,
Women followed their men,
Tending their wounds and all of their needs,
'Camp followers' as they were known then.

But the modern wife, is of a different breed,
In houses, no longer a tent,
A haven for all, a place to make home,
There, til the next posting, sent.

The men, with their duties, at home or away,
In conflict zones, or some foreign war,
On exercise, or in a disaster area, aiding,
In situations never encountered before.

Places to be, places to see, new experiences aplenty,
Adaptability needed, to fit in with new lives,
The children, the camps, the ever changing households,
For the military men, and their loving wives.

"Cabbage"
An allegory of Life (I)

You showed use a cabbage,
A cabbage red, warm, fit for a king,
Was it the Walrus,
who spoke of cabbages, and of many things.

I wonder if it was a red cabbage,
Warm in it's darkness,
A magenta gem glowing,
with a fluorescence all of it's own.

You showed us a cabbage,
I saw a roundness though not a circle,
Satin softness, almost a spongy feel,
Hiding a hard heart.

Leaves with undulating edges,
Like the uneven path of age,
You showed us a cabbage,
It brought me thoughts of Autumn.

Muted colours, golden harvests,
Life preserved in labelled jars,
Mother Nature shedding the old,
Waiting for Spring to awaken the new.

Another cabbage, passed from hand to hand,
For our senses to see and feel,
Still a cabbage, but in a different form,
A piece, a slice, but a whole of that part of the whole.

Rough edged layers,
Deceptive strength,
A strong backbone,
Reaching into purple swirls.

Leaves seen in their innermost hiding places,
Pressed hard, layer upon layer,
Losing their beginning, and their end,
I'm lost, lost in the purple maze.

Turnip
An allegory of Life (II)

Poor, sad looking turnip,
Coarse and ugly,
And yet with unexpected softness,
Perhaps an old turnip,
Where time and circumstance,
Have made the outside hard and bitter,
Though inside there lies a softer core.

A root, tentatively reaching out,
Cut off,
Where once it was the life force,
Is now almost a parasite,
Clinging on to what remains of it's strength,
And yet, though ugly in my sight,
A certain beauty lies in your gnarled shape,
For it is, what's on the inside that matters,
And not that, which on the outside is seen.

ODD VERSES FROM DIFFERENT POEMS

Sunflower

So proud you stood, your face searching
for the sun,
Until, finally, came the first snows of winter,
And bowed your golden head.

....

From "Life's Battlefield"

Here lies peace and tranquillity,
Here lies hope,
Here they lie, are they dead?
No, not dead, only sleeping,
Shell shocked and bleeding,
Afraid.

....

From "Half -forgotten paths"

How careless is our mind's wanderings,
Cannoning down paths of unfulfilled dreams,
Tearing open the heart's treasured packets,
Spilling their contents to life's cold view.

....

Thoughts I

And 'Man' spewed radio-active rose petals,
To fall gently on all children,
Eating out their souls,
Leaving their bodies standing naked in the rain.

....

Thoughts II

What happened to that girl I was,
The free spirit, that now cowers
in one corner of my mind,
So many dead years,
Funny, I thought I was really living then.

....

From "Is this really Love 3"

I've sat and tried to put you into words,
But I cannot,
You are as elusive as one drop of water,
Flowing in a river,
You drift like the mist,
Swirling, but staying nowhere.

....

Birth

Yellow ribbon bedecked bouquet,
Reward for work I've done today,
A brother for Tim, for Chris a son,
And for Simon, a new life begun.

....

Ode to a piece of Cheese

(1974 visit)

I can say, and with great ease,
I've been inside a piece of cheese,
And I'll say, with great propriety,
It's not of a usual variety.

The type of cheese I have in mind,
Is one of the cottage kind,
It even has a door to enter,
And two rooms in the centre.

There are many nutrients you can find,
Some for your body, but most for your mind,
It is filled with priceless treasure,
For you to browse through at your leisure.

In Hastings this cheese is found,
In the Old Town, you must look round,
For it is there, for one who sees,
The cottage called "The Piece of Cheese".

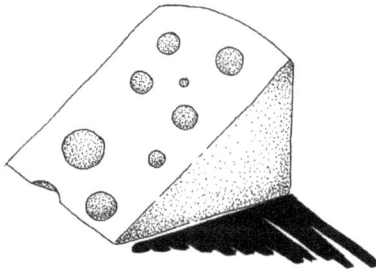

Fleeting Images I

Decisions, not easily come by,
Deciding where to go with my life,
Many thoughts, wine sodden sometimes,
Oft-times grabbed from fleeting images,
Turmoil.

Sitting alone, in crowded rooms,
Waiting, what for,
Is there anything else left on offer,
There must be.
Wondering

Fleeting Images II

Sunshine images, caught for a second in time,
So transitory,
Bursting through my fingers, though I hold so lightly,
Butterfly-like, you came into my life.

I saw your beauty,
Vivid and bright, settling only for a moment
If I try to hold you, will your colours fade,
To be reborn in some other place.

For your Brother

May you live in our hearts and memories,
Ever in our hearts and minds,
Resting in the arms of your beloved country,
Vanquished forever, the ills of life,
Yours is now peace and tranquillity,
Not just for today, but tomorrow and always.

Time can no longer age you,
In our love you now take your rest,
Each dawn and every sun setting,
Returned to the circle of your family,
No more travelling, but home at last,
Ever and always in this land to dwell,
You, our dearly loved brother and son.

Stormy Day

The Wind howled, and the trees swayed,
No leaves to stop it's progress,
Bare branches, naked and exposed,
But defiant in their stance.

The Rain came down in torrents,
Battering against the window panes,
Constantly tapping, beating out a rhythm,
Daring those inside, to come out.

Heavier and heavier, and stronger and stronger,
A winter duel, betwixt wind and rain,
The garden plants reeling under the assault,
Their need for water fully assuaged.

The sky grey and glowering,
A suitable backdrop, whilst Nature has it's play,
Battling, one against the other,
A wild and stormy day.

Days such as these are for reflection,
Whilst warm and dry and safe,
A little like life, with opposing forces,
Who, which and when will the victor decide.

Round one to the Rain.

Stormy Night

The Wind blew hard, then harder,
Ferociously rattling windows and doors,
Whistling through the cracks,
Waking me from my sleep.

Everything in movement,
Like a restless sea,
Covers lifted, flapping in the air,
Like birds making ready for flight.

A moonless sky, dark and heavy,
I hide, whilst in my bed,
Listening to the steady roar of heightening sound,
Trees bending to his will.

The Wind showing his muscle,
Waiting to challenge the Rain,
Their winter duel continued,
Under the cover of night.

The garden in full movement,
The air filled with shrieks and moans,
Flower pots moved from their positions,
In this violent game of chess.

From under my warm bedclothes,
I'm afraid to look, but fascinated too,
The howling, leaving no doubt,
The Wind reinstating it's majesty and might.

A siren sound piercing the night,
The traffic on the bypass slowed,
A fallen tree or something worse,
Lying silently in the dark and cold.

No abating, an hour gone by,
Creaking fences, shuddering from the onslaught,
I worry at what I might see,
What devastation in the morning light.

Round two to the Wind.

Storm's Reign End

The highway lights flickered, and went out,
From my window, I could see,
The Sun on it's westward path, pink then gold,
Pushing away Night, until next he appeared.

The Wind, now quiet, a gentle breeze,
Blowing softly over the land,
It's fighting cousin moved on to another place,
And Rain hidden away in some dark cloud.

The battle done, all forces spent,
An equal contest fought and gone,
The only victors, the nourished blades of grass,
And me, still warm and cosy, in my bed.

The storm's reign ended.

One all, until the next time.

Yellow Bird

I saw her from my window, slim and yellow
High above the trees, moving stealthily between the houses,
Stopping and starting, head bobbing, silently swaying,
Carrying out her day's work.

From mud and bricks and concrete,
Each form taking it's shape,
The yellow bird working so very hard,
Lifting each section into place.

Building nests of different sizes,
Dwellings, box caves, and homes,
For two legged creatures and their offspring,
The next generations to own.

Rising from the ground, layer on layer,
Brick on brick, tile on tile,
Windows, like all seeing eyes, looking out,
Waiting ready for the next settlers to come.

All still now, a proud parent, waiting,
New life, filling up the spaces,
The yellow bird, packed up and moving on,
To where the next nests are to be.

And
Other
Stories

The River

Morning

The last of the city lights go out,
As the first fingers of dawn creep into the sky,
The sun slowly shows his head above the eastern horizon,
Rising steadily until the whole golden globe is on show,
The River, quiet, it's daily toil not yet begun,
The only movement, from the gentle lapping of the waves and the
    birds busy amongst the rock pools looking for food,
Their cries echoing through the air.
Some early morning dog walkers, are as surprised to see me as I
    am to see them.

In the hazy sky the first flights of the day are seen,
Work at the Cargo terminal and the Refinery too,
The River, however is calm and serene, it's deep water channels
    filling, and sandbanks being covered,
in readiness for pilots to bring in the ships from the Bar,
The sun is reflected in the water, a golden path stretching from
    shore to shore,
Quiet for now, but tranquillity soon to be shattered, as the day to
    day life of the River will begin.

Day

The wind blows, ruffling my hair,
Making the waves dance as the tide comes in,
The pier, part submerged, no longer in use,
The pylons, a reminder of what was, and now no longer,
A cargo boat moves slowly up stream,

Avoiding the sand banks, as it looks for it's berth,
Making ready to off-load her precious cargo,
Small boats begin their hourly tasks of ferrying
packets of tourists across the river,
As the Dazzle ship floats by.

The riverside buildings stand tall against the skyline,
The Liver Birds watch whilst the river plies it's trade,
Seagulls, drifting on the wind, hoping to espy,
some juicy morsel, small birds in their wake,
The river fully awakened, power in it's flow,
Aiding the Tugs as they bring in the Tankers,
Two geese fly by, powerful wings flapping, going to
who knows where, and all of the time,
the waves hurl themselves to the shore, crashing against the
    unforgiving sea wall.

Evening

The sun slowly sinks over the horizon and the light fades,
With tinges of dusky pink, and streaks of blue grey,
Birds glide by, looking for their night's roost,
The River, quiet, the Tide having turned,
Leaving exposed sand, rocks and pools,
Lights begin to appear on the skyline,
The Ferry terminal, the Airport and the Promenade,
As I watch, dark shapes of people's lives are illuminated,
Hotels, Cathedrals and Homes,
Reflected in the calm waters.

In my car, radio on, I wait for night to fall,
I look away for a moment, and hundreds of golden lights appear,
    switched on in an instant,
The River, still, like a silver ribbon, stretching out before me, mile
    upon mile,
Plays host to the buoys blinking out their warning lights,
No ships on the water, the day's activity done,

Waiting off the Bar for the next high tide,
As darkness falls more shapes emerge from the gloom,
All along the shoreline.

Night

All quiet, darkness like a velvet blanket,
Lies over the River,
On the far shore, the lights of the City twinkle,
White, red and yellow, and the occasional blue,
Lighting up, the big wheel and the many floored hotels,
The busy metropolis making ready for the night time revels,
The lights reflected all along the coast,
Their colours making paths through the water,
Shimmering patterns of light.

A silent Tanker glides down the River,
Her dark shadow lit only by her bridge,
Across the night air, muffled sounds of traffic can be heard,
And in the far distance, the flames of the Refinery shoot into the
    sky, as the lights there flicker and dance,
A late flight, wing lights blinking, touches down,
Bringing back the holiday makers,
Safe and home,
A solitary man, out walking his old dog, acknowledges me,
As we watch together, the life on our amazing River.

River Mersey

Feline Friends

(All much loved strays and rescue beings - from 1985 to the present).

First came Domino, tiny, half black, half white,
Nestling in my crash helmet,
Brought to her new home, so small, so young,
Yet her hooded eyes, knowing and wise,
My little Lady.

Jasper (Jassy), came next, white with black splodges,
A look of a panda face, when sitting down,
Greatly adventurous, a wandering male,
Sadly disappeared, and never found,
Mourned by all, especially Lady Dom Doms.

Looked after Amber, a foster family,
Sadly far too briefly, though settled and happy,
A scare, a run, collision with a car,
Our beautiful girl gone in a second,
My tortoiseshell beauty.

Quantum Durham then appeared one day,
A short haired ginger Tom, begging for food,
No collar, no ID, and so became ours,
And lived with us until his life was done,
Always known as 'Boy', our little man.

Barnaby followed, officially adopted, my cuddly boy,
Long-haired ginger, with a foot long tail,
Never well, but he fought it bravely,
Happy, in my arms, when his last breath went.
My little lion.

Jet-Lee, from the streets, on a cold November night,
Followed me home, then never left,
My black beauty, with film star looks,
Friendly, loyal and so relaxed,
My laid-back boy.

Woken on a stormy night, by my J-L,
Insistent I open the front door,
Sitting on the step, a soaked, cold, dirty creature,
With eyes that appealed for help,
I let her in.

She became my project, a strange old girl,
Good food, good wash and there emerged,
A soft fluffy black and white, like you see in cartoons,
A grand lady, content to just sit and purr,
I called her 'Chloe face'.

My next little housemate, belonged to my son,
He moved to a flat, so a lodger I had,
Funny little face, with splodges of black and white,
But with beautiful eyes that reached into your soul,
I named her Molly-Kitty.

A visitor, from time to time,
Called in for a snack, a stroke and a sleep,
A wanderer, fluffy, grey and white,
A handsome boy, of regal bearing,
Known to me as Sasha.

Whilst out in the garden, through the fence he came,
A tiny white kitten, about a year old,
Black smudges on his face, my friend called him Pingue,
But to me he was Charlie Sandon,
Gone too soon.

A day later, another kitten appeared,
Completely different, no relation to CS,
I thought there must have been some sort of
'bush telegraph', telling all strays,
Where to come.

A stunning creature, who as he grew,
Took on the look of his wild ancestors,
A tabby with the colours of a tiger, and shape
of a Cheetah, back dipped and powerful legs,
But so affectionate, my magnificent Cairo Lancy.

A phone call asking if I had space for another,
A mostly white tortoiseshell, found lost and alone,
A pretty little girl, massive personality,
Easily holds her own, she lives with me still,
Madame Ellie-May.

Another tabby, to join the household,
Eight weeks old, from a family with dogs,
Handsome, mischievous, defender of our territory,
Loves his Ellie, as she does him,
Now four, and huge, my Mali-Blue.

Another stray, tabby and white,
Battle scarred, old, but with great charm,
His rugged face appeared at the door,
Belonging to no-one, least no-one known,
I gave him food and a name, Devon Lacey.

These amazing beings have been part of my life from the 1980s,
I searched for their owners, but to no avail,
Now chipped, injected and insured,
Each having their time and space,
They share their lives with me,
Until their beautiful eyes close,
I have loved them all.

(My friends call me the Cat Lady, I can't imagine why ...…)

Phone Call

Hello, hello, is that you?
Yes this is me, who's that?
It's me, of course, how are you?
Oh, you know, pretty well,
Just thought I'd ring to see how you are,
That's nice, thanks,
How are things with you?
Oh just the same, always the same,
Anything new with you?
No, like you, just the same,
Seen much of old so and so,
Old so and so?
Yes, you know, that old guy,
Can't say that I have, not for a while anyway,
I expect he's busy,
Yes that must be it,
Lots to do on his allotment,
His allotment? Didn't know he had an allotment.
Who are we talking about here?
Your friend Sam,
I don't have a friend Sam,
Isn't that Frances?
No,
Oh sorry, wrong number ....

The Roadie and the Doorman

What time's the Gig tonight?
OK, pick up time half eight,
Pack the gear, load the lads, off to the venue.

See you later, hope it's a good one,
Instruments and voices in fine form,
Later, back for the de-rig, load up and home.

Oh damn, am late, have to hurry, hope there's a parking place,
   the traffic is so slow, come on!!
A space, thanks, but will have to drive straight in,
No time for manoeuvring.

Well that's 'effing' awful, two feet, at least, from the kerb,
But in the lines, so just about legal,
Lock the doors, about to move out, when a voice comes out of
   the night.

"You're not going to leave that, like that, are you?"
"Well yes, actually, I'm late, doing my duty, transport for the
   band"

"The band?" "Yes, the lads that are playing next door,
tonight".

A disparaging look at my Micra, derision barely contained,
then with disbelief, more comments made.

"You're picking up a band, in that?"
"Yes"
"In that?"

"Yes, not big speakers, but everything else, mixing desk, microphone stand, leads ...."
"How many are there in the band?"
"Three, and me, of course",
"In that",
"Yes, and their instruments. Two guitars and a cajon drum"

Silence, followed by a derisive "let me get this straight, you are going to get all the equipment, instruments, you and three grown men into that!"
"Yes"
"Well, this I have to see"
"Oh, you will"

I can't tell you how much I enjoyed the incredulous look on his face as we loaded up and drove away.

He is my friend now, looks out for me every week, and thankfully my parking skills have improved.

How much more rock and roll can you get, than having an old lady, in a Micra, picking you up.
Not much !!!   Such fun.

The Train

Today is the day, for the journey to begin,
We wait on the platform for the train to arrive,
Expectations high, cases around our feet,
Time to board,
Shown to our cabin,
Our home from home,
For the next week,
Just us and the train.

Food in the lockers, luggage stowed away,
Clothes hung up, untidy already, just like my room,
Books and cameras, drinks and sweets,
Laid out on the table,
Beds partially made,
Seats for the daytime,
Beds for the night,
And we are off.

A clanking and jarring, metal on rails,
The singing of the wheels as they gather speed,
The rocking and rolling, the shudders and creaks,
Out of the station,
Down the tracks,
Past the sidings,
Old rolling stock rusting,
In the cold morning air.

The views from the windows, villages and towns,
Small holdings, ramshackle buildings and farms,
Land for cultivation, no space wasted,
A glimpse of a horse,

A sheep or a cow,
Workers in the fields,
Workers maintaining the line,
Early morning life.

Large birds of prey, gliding on air,
Forgotten train tracks, no longer in use,
Now leading to who knows why or where,
The forests stretch out,
Mile upon mile,
Silhouettes of houses,
Set in the trees,
Pockets of humanity.

The birch trees, gently swaying in the breeze,
The head-scarved women, young and old,
Appearing, silently out of the woods,
Like ghosts,
Waiting for the train
To take them to market,
Their weekly run,
Since the railway came.

We come to a station, small but ornate,
With hawkers aplenty, selling their wares,
Bread, milk and cheese and other goods,
For hungry passengers,
Those quick enough,
To make use of the train stops,
To replenish supplies,
For the rest of the journey.

Darkness is falling, as the train rattles on,
Stars in their thousands, sparkle in the clear skies,
In the distance, the outlines of buildings can be seen,
A larger station,
Outskirts of a city,

Neon signs shimmering,
Another place name,
To strike off the list.

Time for rest, the day's experiences done,
Rocked asleep by the train's movement,
A pleasant, if not quite gentle, lullaby,
Moving through the night,
The air whistling past,
The music of the rails,
Metal on metal,
A train symphony.

From out of the windows, a magnificent sight,
A lake, glistening through early morning mist,
Surrounded by snowy mountain peaks,
An ancient landmark,
Dark, deep and mysterious,
Centuries old,
Filling the view,
As far as the eye can see.

Small fishing villages, hugging it's shores,
An isolated house, occupants working the ground,
An industrial area, refinery maybe,
Chimneys smoking,
Machinery working,
People like ants,
Working so hard,
Snapshots of daily life.

Hour after hour, the train travels onward,
Snaking it's way, over endless terrain,
Another day, another night, though there's plenty to see,
Rivers and bridges,
Passengers leaving,
Some joining anew,

Down to the restaurant car,
To try out the food.

A change of place, scrubland and sand,
The countryside flattens, there is less to see,
Though it still holds the interest, with rare glimpses of life,
Occasional small stations,
Just time to get off,
A stretch of the legs,
The local populace to meet,
A smile, a hello and a photograph taken.

Artists at the stations, plying their wares,
Scenes of the desert, tribesmen and their homes,
A way of life, read of only in books,
Free roaming camels,
Grazing horses,
Drinking from a waterhole,
Traditional Yurts,
And now with trucks, cars and motorbikes.

A large metropolis looms on the horizon,
The capital city, but old fashioned in look,
A jumbled place of 60s styled skyscrapers,
Neon signs flashing,
Car horns sounding,
The station busy,
We join in the melee,
For a short time until the train moves on.

Through border crossings and customs checks,
Through wheel changes, carriage by carriage,
Shunting engines doing their heavy work,
Into a new country,
Using a new rail gauge,
The train rattles on,
New experiences to have,
New sights to see.

The scenery now dramatically changed,
Everywhere people out planting the seeds,
Every inch cultivated, many people to feed.
Isolated housing,
Giving way,
To hundreds of tower blocks,
Purposefully built,
Grey against the sky.

The final station, and people galore,
We gather our luggage, and step off into the heat,
Looking for a taxi, to our temporary home,
Through the back streets,
Busy little shops,
Colours, cars, rickshaws and noise,
So, so, many people,
Then, we are here, at last.

Trans Siberian / Trans Mongolian Train
Moscow - Ulan Baatar – Beijing

Road Song *(a traveller's tale)*

Split to Dubrovnik 1968

The coast road ahead, flooded and impassable,
All vehicles redirected up into the hills,
Snuggled in the back of the car,
Wedged in between the rucksacks and a guitar,
I watch the scenery fly by.

My companion, conversing with the driver,
Who had picked up, two tired hitch-hikers,
Taking us on to the next part of our journey,
Now with a slight detour, or so we thought,
In reality, many miles and many hours.

Up in the hills, the road became narrow,
Then almost a track,
With few passing places,
No-one willing to give way, hour after hour,
An old-fashioned stand off.

Frustration seeped in, good natured at first,
But after a while, the horn blowing began,
Angry drivers, out of their cars,
Shouting, arms waving, the air turning 'blue',
Beneath the hot afternoon sun.

The noise, quiet at first, soon rose to a crescendo,
As rage was played out on the horns,
Different cars, different sounds, a roadside tune,
Played out in perfect harmony,
The song of the hills.

I was glad to relax, but not so our fiery driver,
Who waved and shouted with the rest,
Though we were in no rush, that did not apply to him,
Places to be, people to see,
I just sat back and enjoyed the scenery.

Finally it was our turn to move,
Slowly at first, then the track widened out,
The sun, by now, starting to set,
We did not speak, but watched silently,
As the light began to fade.

As the sun dipped below the horizon,
The lights of the vehicles switched on,
Hundreds of cars, snaking down the hillside,
Gathering speed, by degrees,
Down towards the now cleared coast road.

What a sight, a slow moving dragon,
Lit red and white, meandering through the countryside,
Headlights and tail lights,
Making patterns against the now dark sky,
Quiet, the music long gone, the day's adventure done.

Time to part, we said our goodbyes,
And sat at the roadside, for our next lift,
We talked about our day's events,
The frustrations, the anger, then the relief,
But mostly about our dragon and the song.

Realization

I was confident that I was special enough, in my own way, to win
the 'golden' ticket for the Welsh leg of the World Rally Series.
An entrance ticket and the chance to ride the circuit with
reigning champion, and legend, Sebastian Loeb.

I applied, enthusiasm and positivity levels high.
I waited for the prize.
Thought I would re-watch some of the other stages on the TV.
Such excitement, thrills and spills,
Adrenaline pumping through my veins.
I felt every bump in the road, every swerve, smelt the hot tyres on
the gravel,
Listened avidly to every instruction and watched every fast turn
of the wheel.

My attention strayed to the crowd,
Handsome men and beautiful women,
All ages, all equally elegant,
Wrapped up in the excitement of the race
And all, I expected, applying for that special ticket.

I stared at the screen, and suddenly I felt very foolish.
Realization hit me very hard,
What chance did I have, an old lady, no fashion sense,
with teenage style dreams of speed and being on the edge of
danger.

I suddenly felt my age, and did not win, of course,
But I suppose on the plus side, it made me be more realistic about
my choices, and my sense of where I fitted in the world.

The following year Monsieur Loeb retired from the Rally Driving
    circuit,
So the thrill of travelling with him, faded into the realms of what
    might have been.

But some positives have remained, the knowledge that there are
    many things to do and see,
Still a strong desire to experience all things new,
And the final realization that everyone is special in their own
    unique way,
It is just a matter of sorting your dreams,
Oh, and looking for the next 'golden ticket'.

Plans

Plans for the future,
Made from the past,
Plans for strangers, family and friends,
Plans full of wonderment, interest and joy,
Plans for the children, each girl and boy.

Plans carried out resolutely,
New beginnings made,
Plans, firm foundations to lay,
Plans full of questions, some worry, some strife
But overriding all, plans made for life.

This is your life, enjoy it.

Post Script

Knowledge, Understanding, Sympathy
and Empathy.

An exciting and interesting life thus far
and looking forward to whatever comes next.

My thanks to all those I have known and who have enriched my time, to Simon and Penny for all of their support in everything, to Lez for the illustrations, to Karen, Adrienne, and Collette for listening patiently. To family and friends who are an integral part of my life and my honour to know.

Cover photograph "Reflections"
Inside cover "Shoreline"
End photograph "Sunset"
All photographs by Nina Olsson
All Illustrations by Lez Harvey

Book cover artwork by Lez Harvey

To Tamsin, Becky and the team at Grosvenor House Publishing for all of their help, support, advice and encouragement.

www.ingramcontent.com/pod-product-compliance
Lightning Source LLC
LaVergne TN
LVHW070013090426
835508LV00048B/3386